Bible Crosswords

Collection #1

Compiled and Edited
by *Toni Sortor*

A Barbour Book

PUZZLE 1

ACROSS CLUES

2. _____ of Judea. (Matt. 2:1)
8. They rose _____ early. (Num. 14:40)
10. Oxford English Dictionary (abbr.).
11. Emergency Room (abbr.).
13. Melchisedec, king of _____. (Heb. 7:1)
15. Ahad called _____. (1 Kgs. 18:3)
16. This is the way, walk ye in _____. (Isa. 30:21)
17. That we may _____ and believe. (Mark 15:32)
20. For by _____ were all things created. (Col. 1:16)
21. The _____ appeareth, and the tender grass sheweth itself. (Prov. 27:25)
23. Temptress.
24. Decays.
25. _____ and Ma.
27. _____ the cross.

28. Who smote _____ the son of
Jerubbesheth? (2 Sam. 11:21)
31. _____ it not written? (Mark
11:17)
32. _____ angel of the Lord. (Judg.
6:11)
33. Each (abbr.).
34. Saul of _____.
35. Ye seek me, _____. (John 6:26)
36. Either/ _____.
37. This was _____ of whom I
spake. (John 1:15)
39. I in them, and thou in _____.
(John 17:23)
40. Abraham took a wife, and her
name was _____. (Gen. 25:1)

DOWN CLUES

1. Liquid of decay.
2. In the wilderness of _____.
(Gen. 21:14)
3. _____ and fro.
4. David was one.
5. 450 (Roman).

6. Hello (informal).
7. Without _____ ye can do
nothing. (John 15:5)
9. _____, and Medes. . . . (Acts 2:9)
12. Belonging to the son of Bani.
(Neh. 3:17)
14. Rachel. . .called his name _____.
(Gen. 30:8)
18. Masculine object (German).
19. Printer's measure.
22. _____ ye have. . .received Christ
Jesus. (Col. 2:6)
24. A _____ caught in a thicket.
(Gen. 22:13)
25. Sewing fasteners.
26. Before Christ (abbr.).
27. Olive and sunflower.
29. The son of Abinoam. (Judg. 4:6)
30. Sidon. . .and _____. (Gen. 10:15)
34. Open _____ door.
35. National Rifle Association
(abbr.).
36. This _____ that.
38. For example (abbr.).

PUZZLE 2

Mary Ann Freeman

ACROSS CLUES

1. Zilpah's first son. (Gen. 30:11)
4. Exclamation said when making a mistake.
8. Doth the wild ass ______ when he hath grass? (Job 6:5)
12. I and my Father are ______'. (John 10:30)
13. The truth shall make you ______. (John 8:32)
14. They put on him a purple ______. (John 19:2)
15. Deoxyribonucleic acid.
16. ______ my lambs. (John 21:15)
17. Poems intended to be sung.
18. Abram's wife. (Gen. 16:1)
20. For fear that.
22. The ______ of violence is in their hands. (Isa. 59:6)
24. Belonging to a Jericho woman. (Josh. 2:1)
28. All-terrain vehicle.
31. The mother of all living. (Gen. 3:20)
33. Abram's father. (Gen. 11:26)
34. Chemical (abbr.).
36. The rich man was ______. (Mark 10:22)
38. Uncommon.
39. Attempts.
41. And take away all thy ______. (Isa. 1:25)
43. Thirteenth letter of the Hebrew alphabet.
44. Before twilight.
46. Doth not your master ______ tribute? (Matt. 17:24)
48. Potato.

50. Neither hot nor cold.
54. Siamese.
57. Biblical liquid measure.
59. Sweetened lemon drink.
60. Very small amount.
61. Telephone ______ code.
62. National Education Association.
63. Sun at evening.
64. ______ not unto thine own understanding. (Prov. 3:5)
65. One of the twelve tribes. (Ex. 1:4)

DOWN CLUES

1. No other ______ before me. (Ex. 20:3)
2. Prophetess. (Luke 2:36)
3. As ______ children. (Eph. 5:1)
4. All members have not the same ______. (Rom. 12:4)
5. Mineral.
6. ______ an orange.
7. Passover feast.
8. Closer than a ______. (Prov. 18:24)
9. Thy ______ and thy staff. (Ps. 23:4)
10. Lincoln.
11. Yea.
19. Associate in Arts (abbr.).
21. ______ down on the right hand of God. (Heb. 10:12)
23. Televisions.
25. Biblical name for Syria.
26. John ______ witness of him. (John 1:15)
27. Noah's son. (Gen. 6:10)
28. New Testament book.
29. Through (informal).
30. Blood vessel.
32. Desired to ______ this passover. (Luke 22:15)

35. I know that ______ cometh. (John 4:25)
37. That he may ______ the tip of his finger. (Luke 16:24)
40. September (abbr.).
42. He rebuked David. (2 Sam. 12:1-12)
45. Son of Japheth. (1 Chron. 1:5)
47. Seek ______ first the kingdom of God. (Matt. 6:33)
49. Some would even ______ to die. (Rom. 5:7)
51. ______ of remorse.
52. Thought.
53. The ______ in Christ shall rise. (1 Thes. 4:16)
54. ______ the season to be jolly.
55. To cultivate.
56. Ma Bell.
58. Hot beverage.

PUZZLE 3

ACROSS CLUES

1. Daniel the ______. (Matt. 24:15)
7. ______ stilled the people. (Num. 13:30)
12. Lord, ______ long? (Isa. 6:11)
13. Iron ______.
14. Not live by bread ______. (Matt. 4:4)
15. ______ I my brother's keeper? (Gen. 4:9)
16. The family of ______. (1 Sam. 10:21)
17. Measure of weight.
18. A pharaoh.
20. Middle Atlantic state (abbr.).
22. ______ will we sing. (Ps. 21:13)
23. I am ______ the Father. (John 14:10)
24. How ______ it that ye have no faith (Mark 4:40)
25. Go up ______ Jerusalem. (Acts 25:9)
26. Old Testament (abbr.).
27. Saint (abbr.).
28. That it shall ______. (Acts 27:25)
29. Social Security (abbr.).
30. Yes (Spanish).
31. Samuel ran to ______. (1 Sam. 3:5)
33. He looked on the ______. (Num. 24:21)
36. Variation of *aeon*.
37. And the Lord shut him ______. (Gen. 7:16)
38. To scheme. (2 words)
40. Disc jockeys (abbr.).
42. ______ he is come. (John 4:25)
43. Long ______.
45. To the slaughter, like ______. (Jer. 51:40)
46. Christ ______ me. (1 Cor. 1:17)
48. Elimelch's wife. (Ruth 1:2)
50. Standard in golf.
51. Long, narrow fish.
53. Type of acid.
55. Nos.
56. Orderly.
57. Mine enemy and my ______ (sing.) (Ps. 27:2)

DOWN CLUES

1. A certain ______ besought him. (Luke 11:37)
2. Art thou a ______? (Acts 22:27)
3. Exclamation of pain.
4. Houses.
5. Periods of time.
6. Asian holiday.
7. ______ and Abel.
8. American League (abbr.).
9. ______ sat in the gate of Sodom. (Gen. 19:1)
10. Seth called his son's name ______. (Gen. 4:26)
11. Name Rachel called Benjamin. (Gen. 35:18)
19. ______ thou on my right hand. (Matt. 22:44)
21. ______ coat of many colors.
25. Number of lepers. (Luke 17:12)
27. All manner of ______. (Matt. 12:31)
28. The sons of Rachel; Joseph, and ______. (Gen. 35:24)
29. Put away (on a boat).
32. ______ ago.
33. Passest over the brook ______. (1 Kgs. 2:37)

34. Consider ______ in thine heart. (Deut. 4:39)
35. Let us not _____, as do others. (1 Thes. 5:6)
39. Was one _____ a prophetess. (Luke 2:36)
41. I will _____ all thy borders with frogs. (Ex. 8:2)
43. So be it.

44. The _____ true God. (John 17:3)
47. The _____ of life. (Rev. 22:2)
49. The _____ wherein Ishmael had cast...the dead. (Jer. 41:9)
52. Each (abbr.).
54. Egyptian god.
58. Be like a _____ planted by the rivers of water... (Ps. 1:3)

PUZZLE 4

ACROSS CLUES

2. Charge _____, and encourage him. (Deut. 3:28)
8. Terrorist.
9. Ye shall be _____ gods. (Gen. 3:5)
10. I _____ _____ pleasant bread. (Dan. 10:3; 2 words)
13. To _____ or not to _____.
14. Second book of the Bible.
16. Past.
18. He shall cry unto _____ (Ps. 89:26)
19. The Lord saved Hezekiah... from..._____. (2 Chron. 32:22)
24. Ascending up _____ Jerusalem.
25. I will let down the _____. (Luke 5:5)
26. _____ the Baptist.
28. First book of the Bible.
30. Rolled back the stone from the _____. (Matt. 28:2)
32. Yes (Spanish).
33. Buddy.

35. O.T. books of the Bible.
37. A grain often used for cereal.
40. I _____ that I _____.
42. O foolish _____. (Gal. 3:1)
45. _____ Lord and _____ God.
46. Made himself of _____ reputa-
    tion. (Phil. 2:7)
47. So be it.
48. These are the three _____ of
    Noah. (Gen. 9:19)

DOWN CLUES

1. Long _____.
2. A son of Issachar. (Gen. 46:13)
3. They shall be _____ flesh. (Gen.
   2:24)
4. Minor prophet.
5. We. ·
6. Take up thy _____. (Matt. 9:6)
7. The wringing of the _____
   bringeth blood (Prov. 30:33)
10. Implement for cutting down
    trees.
11. Organized travel.
12. Fourth book of the Bible.
15. Postscript (abbr.).
16. _____ angel of the Lord. (Luke
    1:11)
17. Ocean (abbr.).
20. Behold, a man of _____. (Acts
    8:27)
21. Prefix for *not*.
22. Tenth book of the New Testa-
    ment.
23. That I am _____ the Father.
    (John 14:10)
26. A son of Leah. (Gen. 35:23)
27. Last book of the Bible (abbr.).
29. _____ no more. (John 5:14)
31. Egyptian sun god.
34. Rich soil.
36. Belonging to Sam.
38. They..._____ the sacrifices of the
    dead. (Ps. 106:28)
39. A metal.
41. _____ name is Legion. (Mark
    5:9)
42. _____ thy way; thy son liveth.
    (John 4:50)
43. Note on the scale.
44. Yet _____ as by fire. (1 Cor.
    3:15)

PUZZLE 5

Mary Ann Freeman

ACROSS CLUES

1. Touched the _____ . (Matt. 9:20)
4. I know in _____. (1 Cor. 13:12)
8. Sendeth _____ on the just. (Matt. 5:45)
12. The serpent beguiled _____. (2 Cor. 11:3)
13. _____ despised his birthright. (Gen. 25:34)
14. Woe to them that are at _____ in Zion (Amos 6:1)
15. _____ as a sheep to the slaughter. (Acts 8:32)
16. I will give you _____. (Matt. 11:28)
17. As the Lord _____. (Josh. 11:9)
18. I _____ toward the mark. (Phil. 3:14)
20. Now abideth faith, _____, charity. (1 Cor. 13:13)
22. Your life is _____ with Christ in God. (Col. 3:3)
24. This is the _____ of John. (John 1:19)
28. They called for Jesus' death.
31. All things _____ possible. (Mark 9:23)
33. Where Joshua and all Israel stoned Achan. (Josh. 7:24-25)
34. A tenth of an ephah. (Ex. 16:36)
36. Verily I say unto _____.
38. Say ye unto your brethren, _____. (Hos. 2:1)
39. Moses' brother. (Ex. 4:14)
41. National Security Council (abbr.).
43. Labor Day month (abbr.).
44. How Samuel's sons were influenced. (1 Sam. 8:3)
46. _____ hath not seen. (1 Cor. 2:9)
48. Ahab served _____ a little. (2 Kgs. 10:18)
50. If thy _____ eye offend thee. (Matt. 5:29)
54. Run with patience the _____. (Heb. 12:1)
57. I am the true _____. (John 15:1)
59. Japanese drama.
60. The twelfth month. (Es. 3:7)
61. Seared with a hot _____. (1 Tim. 4:2)
62. Solomon's navy brought him this animal. (1 Kgs. 10:22)
63. The son of _____. (Mark 6:3)
64. _____ any of you. (1 Cor. 6:1)
65. Were there not _____ cleansed? (Luke 17:17)

DOWN CLUES

1. _____ thou mine unbelief. (Mark 9:24)
2. Sing of the mercies of the Lord for _____. (Ps. 89:1)
3. Darius' nationality. (Dan. 11:1)
4. Cyrus king of _____. (2 Chron. 36:23)
5. Indicates an enzyme.
6. Be not _____ with thy mouth. (Ec. 5:2)
7. Private instructor.
8. Isaac's wife. (Rom. 9:10)
9. Auto club.
10. Independent School District (abbr.).
11. Indicates maiden name.
19. Be quiet!
21. Green vegetable.
23. O ye _____ bones. (Ez. 37:4)
25. Electrical units.
26. Bear witness also at _____. (Acts 23:11)
27. To shed drops.
28. Ruth left this country. (Ruth 1:22)

29. One of the sons of Eliphaz. (Gen. 36:11)
30. One of the sons of Zophah. (1 Chron. 7:36)
32. Long time.
35. Thought it not _____ to be equal with God. (Phil. 2:6)
37. Them which despitefully _____ you. (Matt. 5:44)
40. National Education Association (abbr.).
42. They found a man of _____. (Matt. 27:32)
45. Jesse's youngest son. (1 Sam. 17:14)
47. East Indies (abbr.).
49. Italian money.
51. Which strain at a _____. (Matt. 23:24)
52. The _____ of glory. (Col. 1:27)
53. _____ that which is in part shall be done away. (1 Cor. 13:10)
54. Abraham went and took the _____. (Gen. 22:13)
55. American Dental Association (abbr.).
56. Automobile.
58. Neither cold _____ hot. (Rev. 3:16)

PUZZLE 6

David Greenlee

ACROSS CLUES

1. I _____ (name of God).
4. Father.
6. A deity or idol.
9. Fruit of the Spirit. (Gal. 5:22)
13. Satan went _____ and fro. (Job 1:7)
14. Small, humanlike mythical being.
15. Prefix of negation.
16. _____ from God the Father. (Gal. 1:3)
18. Moses' second book (abbr.).
19. _____, every one that thirsteth (Isa. 55:1)
20. _____ fell from Saul's eyes. (Acts 9:18)
23. Peter wrote _____ the scattered Jews. (1 Pet. 1:1)
24. I will...have mercy on _____. (Jer. 33:26)
25. Indefinite singular article.

26. Hiram's navy brought this animal to Solomon. (1 Kgs. 10:22)
27. Traveled with Rebekah. (Gen. 24:59)
29. Ancient city.
31. The Spirit descended in this form. (Matt. 3:16)
33. This animal spoke to Balaam. (Num. 22:28)
34. In him is _____ darkness. (1 John 1:5)
35. Used to kill Stephen. (Acts 7:58)
37. Pilate found no _____ of death in Jesus. (Luke 23:22)
39. Relationship of Martha and Mary to Lazarus. (John 11:1)
41. _____ his money. (Gen. 42:27)
42. Built the ark. (Luke 17:27)
45. Peleth's son. (Num. 16:1)
47. Year of the Lord (Latin abbr.).
48. Ye shall be _____ gods. (Gen. 3:5)
49. Love thy _____. (Matt. 5:43)

DOWN CLUES

1. Albert (short form).
2. Something small in the eye.
3. King of Bashan. (Num. 21:33)
4. King of Assyria. (2 Kgs. 15:19)
5. Set your _____ on the things above. (Col. 3:2, plural)
6. Fruit of the Spirit. (Gal. 5:22)
7. Gold (Spanish).
8. Eats.
10. A just and perfect man. (Gen. 6:9)
11. The pure in heart...shall _____ God. (Matt. 5:8)
12. Fruit of the Spirit. (Gal. 5:22)
16. Sound in faith, charity, and _____. (Titus 2:2)
17. Jesus was moved with _____. (Matt. 9:36)
21. _____, Lord God! (Jer. 4:10)
22. Ostrichlike bird.
25. Donkey.
26. Alabama (abbr.).
28. Brought food to Elijah. (1 Kgs. 17:6)
30. My soul _____ in the Lord. (Ps. 34:2)
31. It is lawful to _____ well. (Matt. 12:12)
32. Rebekah's face covering. (Gen. 24:65, modern spelling)
36. Golf ball supporter.
38. Opposite of down.
40. Lion's call. (1 Pet. 5:8)
43. Name of an altar. (Josh. 22:34)
44. See 3 down.
45. 21-verse prophet (abbr.).
46. If we say we have _____ sin. (1 John 1:8)

PUZZLE 7
Diana Rowland

ACROSS CLUES

1. Now the Lord said unto ______.
   (Gen. 12:1)
6. Are not ______ and Pharpar rivers
   of Damascus? (2 Kgs. 5:12)
11. Abraham...______ the wood.
    (Gen. 22:3)
12. Athenian woman who believed.
    (Acts 17:34)
15. In charge of King Ahasuerus'
    women. (Es. 2:3)
16. The Lord sent him to meet Moses
    in the wilderness. (Ex. 4:27)
17. Infant's first word for *Daddy.*
18. Joseph's wife. (Gen. 41:45)
20. The works that are done ______
    the sun. (Ec. 1:14)
22. I am, you are, he______.
23. Dialect for *get.*
24. Eli heard the noise of the ______.
    (1 Sam. 4:14)
25. Joshua sent men from Jericho to
    ______. (Josh. 7:2)
26. Descendants of Eri. (Num. 26:16)
28. Sarah shall bear unto thee ______
    this set time. (Gen. 17:21)
29. Not bow down thyself to them,
    ______ serve them. (Ex. 20:5)
31. I ______ the marathon.
32. Place of 12 wells of water.
    (Ex. 15:27)
34. ______ ye therefore. (Matt. 28:19)
35. The sons of Aaron, took either of
    them his ______. (Lev. 10:1)
37. They went forth ______ go.
    (Gen. 12:5)
38. King of Greek gods.
40. Cut off his right ______.
    (Luke 22:50)

41. God said, ______ shall not eat of
    every tree. (Gen. 3:1)
42. Bright ______.
44. Strong people set in battle
    ______. (Joel 2:5)
46. And, ______, the angel of the
    Lord came. (Luke 2:9)
47. Melts.
49. Upon the great ______ of their
    right feet. (Lev. 8:24)
52. For it is the ______ of ______
    flesh. (Lev. 17:14; 2 words)
54. Ahian, and Schechem, and
    ______. (1 Chron. 7:19)
55. Led him away to ______ first.
    (John 18:13)
56. An ______ ______ the hole (2 words).

DOWN CLUES

1. Gallio was the deputy of ______.
   (Acts 18:12)
2. Thou shalt be a ______.
   (Gen. 12:2)
3. Why do the heathen ______?
   (Ps. 2:1)
4. The Lord is the ______ of all
   such. (1 Thes. 4:6)
5. ______, myself, and I.
6. And ______ bare Jabal.
   (Gen. 4:20)
7. Candy or ice cream ______.
8. Loves.
9. Mary Poppins was one.
10. Pass over through ______.
    (Deut. 2:18)
13. Joseph's brothers didn't know
    his ______.
14. "Hey, ______." Beetle Bailey's
    call.
16. Dresses (verb).
19. The fowl of the ______.
    (Gen. 1:26)
21. The sun ______ of Ahaz.
    (Isa. 38:8)

24. And the _____ of pure gold.
(1 Kgs. 7:50)
27. You get this at a beach.
30. Leak out slowly.
32. Flighty, capricious.
33. _____, Larry, and Curly.
35. The tents of _____ in affliction.
(Hab. 3:7)
36. Give _____ to his commandments. (Ex. 15:26)
39. Hast thou _____ of the tree?
(Gen. 3:11)
42. So that it went _____ with
Moses. (Ps. 106:32)

43. The noise of them that sing
_____ _____ hear. (Ex. 32:18;
2 words)
44. Pointed tools for piercing holes.
45. Broken the bands of your _____.
(Lev. 26:13)
48. Order _____ _____ carte (2 words).
50. Benjamin's son. (Gen. 46:21)
51. Cleanseth us from all _____.
(1 John 1:7)
53. Do, Re, Mi, _____.
54. Syllable to sing when you don't
know the words.

PUZZLE 8

Mary Ann Freeman

ACROSS CLUES

1. Pick up your _____.
   (John 5:8 NIV)
4. Go _____ to thy friends.
   (Mark 5:19)
8. Mary hath chosen that good
   _____. (Luke 10:42)
12. Many _____ called.
    (Matt. 22:14)
13. A garden eastward in _____.
    (Gen. 2:8)
14. The Eranites came from _____.
    (Num. 26:36)
15. Likened unto _____ virgins.
    (Matt. 15:1)
16. Part of a necklace.
17. The veil...was _____ in twain.
    (Matt. 27:51)
18. _____ Tots (brand name).
20. Turn and _____. (Isa. 22:18)
22. For the sky is _____. (Matt. 16:2)
24. The third day he shall be _____
    again. (Matt. 17:23)
28. Who Matthew would work for
    today.
31. Harder to be _____ than a strong
    city. (Prov. 18:19)
33. The Lord added to the church
    _____. (Acts 2:47)
34. Lament.
36. My _____ shall supply.
    (Phil. 4:19)
38. Thy _____ is as the tower of
    Lebanon. (Song of Sol. 7:4)
39. Scourge a man that is a _____?
    (Acts 22:25)
41. In the beginning _____ the
    Word. (John 1:1)
43. Nickname for Edward.
44. That I may _____ unto you.
    (Rom. 1:11)
46. Your yea be yea; and your
    _____, _____. (Jam. 5:12)
48. Call me not Naomi, call me
    _____. (Ruth 1:20)
50. Goodness and _____. (Ps. 23:6)
54. In _____ was there a voice
    heard. (Matt. 2:18)
57. _____ was a cunning hunter.
    (Gen. 25:27)
59. International Labor Organization
    (abbr.).
60. Worthy to _____ the book.
    (Rev. 5:2)
61. Ireland.
62. Country northeast of India
    (abbr.).
63. Belonging to Rachel's youngest
    son (nickname). (Gen. 35:18)
64. _____, why persecutest thou me?
    (Acts 9:4)
65. The light of the body is the
    _____. (Matt. 6:22)

DOWN CLUES

1. Gospel name (abbr.).
2. Length times width.
3. Enlarge the place of thy _____.
   (Isa. 54:2)
4. Nurse of the _____ women.
   (Ex. 2:7)
5. Poem.
6. Strong _____ belongeth to them.
   (Heb. 5:14)
7. A familiar spirit at _____.
   (1 Sam. 28:7)
8. Cyrus the _____. (Dan. 6:28)
9. Ye _____ the branches.
   (John 15:5)
10. Esau _____ to meet him.
    (Gen. 33:4)
11. Explosive.
19. A son of Judah. (Num. 26:19)
21. He was _____. (Mark 10:22)
23. A living _____ is better than a
    dead lion. (Ec. 9:4)
25. I lay in _____. (1 Pet. 2:6)

26. Children, or ______ I die.
(Gen. 30:1)
27. Bring rams' skins ______ red.
(Ex. 25:5)
28. Father of Omri. (1 Chron. 9:4)
29. No ______ for them. (Luke 2:7)
30. Corn mush.
32. ______ is the day of salvation
(2 Cor. 6:2)
35. Belonging to the captain of the
king of Syria. (2 Kgs. 5:1)
37. Bilhah's first son. (Gen. 30:5-6)
40. National Rifle Association
(abbr.).
42. Moses and ______ stood before
me. (Jer. 15:1)

45. All the ______ of the field.
(Isa. 55:12)
47. All ______ people. (Ps. 47:1)
49. They which dwelt in ______
heard the word. (Acts 19:10)
51. The harvest of the earth is
______. (Rev. 14:15)
52. Hath not the potter power over
the ______? (Rom. 9:21)
53. My ______ is easy. (Matt. 11:30)
54. Will a man ______ God?
(Mal. 3:8)
55. To mimic.
56. Fishers of ______. (Mark 1:17)
58. Islands east of Indonesia.

PUZZLE 9

Diana Rowland

ACROSS CLUES

1. I will raise unto David a righteous _____. (Jer. 23:5)
7. If any be a _____ of the word. (Jam. 1:23)
13. An ocean-edge lake.
14. _____ for thy life. (Gen. 19:17)
15. Ivory and _____. (Ezek. 27:15)
16. Of _____ shall there be _____ like weight. (Ex. 30:34; 2 words)
17. That I might not _____ against thee. (Ps. 119:11)
18. Who walk in the _____ of the Lord. (Ps. 119:1)
21. Pay _____ view.
22. Temporary duty (abbr.).
23. Could not drink of the waters of _____. (Ex. 15:23)
25. And I will walk _____ liberty. (Ps. 119:45)
27. Accompanied him into Asia _____ of Berea. (Acts 20:4)
29. Delayed not _____ keep thy commandments. (Ps. 119:60)
30. Thy law _____ my delight. (Ps. 119:77)
32. _____ Naomi's husband died. (Ruth 1:3)
34. And _____ them, and _____ them down with ease. (Judg. 20:43; 2 words)
36. Halah, and Habor, and _____. (1 Chron. 5:26)
37. _____ Jerusalem...as a _____ doth gather. (Luke 13:34; 2 words)
38. And Peleg lived after he begat _____. (Gen. 11:19)
41. _____, and Shema, and Moladah. (Josh. 15:26)

42. Nickname for Edward.
43. _____ and feather.
44. They assigned _____ in the wilderness. (Josh. 20:8)
46. Three wise men of Christmas.
47. Hear _____ Israel: . . .to _____ in . . ._____ shalt thou drive them out. (Deut. 9:1, 3; 3 words)
48. I shall keep _____ unto the end. (Ps. 119:33)
50. A little _____ in _____ cruse. (1 Kgs. 17:12; 2 words)
51. The region of _____; ...daughter of Solomon _____ wife. (1 Kgs. 4:11; 2 words)
52. They also do _____ iniquity. (Ps. 119:3)
53. And for our little _____. (Ezra 8:21)

DOWN CLUES

1. Hallowed.
2. Furious.
3. And being in an _____ he prayed. (Luke 22:44)
4. Prefix meaning "not."
5. Shy.
6. Head nurse (abbr.).
7. And _____ heard me. (Ps. 120:1)
8. East-southeast (abbr.).
9. Not a hat, but _____ baseball _____ (2 words).
10. The _____ is not to the swift. (Ec. 9:11)
11. Caleb took unto him _____. (1 Chron. 2:19)
12. Rural Electrification Administration (abbr.).
18. Deborah...the wife of _____ (h). (Judg. 4:4)
19. Geshur, and _____, with _____ towns. (1 Chron. 2:23; 2 words)
20. And _____ the whole face of the ground. (Gen. 2:6)

23. The snail, and the _____.
(Lev. 11:30)
24. Eliab the son of _____.
(Num. 2:7)
26. _____ day.
27. Child's TV program.
28. Bright color.
30. Eli's grandson. (1 Sam. 4:21)
31. Whither shall I cause my _____
to _____? (2 Sam. 13:13;
2 words)
33. A _____ man had two sons,
(Luke 15:11)
35. Not come _____ _____ upon mine
head. (Judg. 16:17; 2 words).
39. Doth the _____ mount up?
(Job 39:27)
40. That had been the wife of _____.
(Matt. 1:6)
45. Kanga's child.
46. Sound made by a cow.
48. Thy word have I had _____ my
heart. (Ps. 119:11)
49. Make me _____ understand.
(Ps. 119:27)

PUZZLE 10

ACROSS CLUES

1. To carry something.
4. Call thy land ______ ah (Isa. 62:4)
8. Shish______ob.
10. Seen his star in the ______.
    (Matt. 2:2)
11. Him only shalt thou ______.
    (Matt. 4:10)
13. To go on a ______.
14. Also.
15. Thy word... I will ______ it.
    (Ps. 119:105-106)
18. Anna (var.).
19. Just a little bit.
20. Samuel ran unto ______.
    (1 Sam. 3:5)
21. Printer's measure.
23. That my joy might ______ in you.
    (John 15:11)
25. Gives medicine to.
27. In the country of ______.
    (1 Kgs. 4:19)
29. Praises.
31. A little while, and ye shall not
    ______ me. (John 16:16)
32. To tie a rope off.
33. As he ______ pure. (1 John 3:3)
34. Not B.C.
35. They ______ the ship aground.
    (Acts 27:41)
36. To exist.
38. Give ______, all ye inhabitants.
    (Joel 1:2)
39. Parent Teacher Association
    (abbr.).
40. A two year college degree.
41. Medical specialty (abbr.).
43. To rest.
45. Better...he were ______ into the
    sea. (Mark 9:42)
46. Or the ______, be not darkened.
    (Ec. 12:2)
47. I have fed you with ______.
    (1 Cor. 3:2)
48. Professional engineer (abbr.).

DOWN CLUES

1. To sit or ___ ______. (2 words)
2. For there are set ______ of
   judgment. (Ps. 122:5)
3. Mommy (var.).
4. Thou shalt not ______ false
   witness. (Ex. 20:16)
5. What cannibals do.
6. Teach Judah the ______ of the
   bow. (2 Sam. 1:18)
7. Light (abbr.).
8. When I ______ silence. (Ps. 32:3)
9. Or touch the ______. (Ex. 19:12)
12. Length of time.
13. To perform something.
16. Cut off his right ______.
    (Luke 22:50)
17. Lord of lords, and ______ of kings.
    (Rev. 17:14)
22. Cast the ______ on the right side
    of the ship. (John 21:6)
24. When fowls came Abram drove
    them ______ (Gen. 15:11)
26. Ephlal begat ______.
    (1 Chron. 2:37)
27. Office of Strategic Services
    (abbr.).
28. ______ men that were lepers.
    (Luke 17:12)
29. Thy word is a ______ unto my
    feet. (Ps. 119:105)
30. That we may ______ with him.
    (John 11:16)

31. Jesus _____.
32. So shall thy _____ be filled.
(Prov. 3:10)
35. Egyptian sun god.
36. Rolled _____ the stone.
(Matt. 28:2)
37. Jesus also suffered without the
_____. (Heb. 13:12)
38. Estimated Time of Arrival
(abbr.).
40. Snake.
42. New Testament (abbr.).
44. Not A.M.

PUZZLE 11

ACROSS CLUES

1. Hannah's son. (1 Sam. 1:20)
5. For _____ persecuted they the prophets. (Matt. 5:12)
7. Spirit of the Lord came up _____ David. (1 Sam. 16:13)
8. John also was baptizing in _____ near to Salim. (John 3:23)
10. The promise is ... to all that are _____ off. (Acts 2:39)
12. An explosive.
13. The _____ of God. (Ps. 46:4)
15. A great _____ dragon. (Rev. 12:3)
17. Whose son is _____? (Matt. 22:42)
18. How long is it _____ since this came unto him? (Mark 9:21)
19. Either/_____.
21. Hated.
23. A little bear.
25. _____ it not written? (Mark 11:17)
27. I have never _____ any thing common (Acts 10:14)
30. That they might have life more _____. (John 10:10)
34. To be a certain place.
35. The director _____ the play.
36. A carnivore _____ meat.
39. Printer's measure.
41. Call for the elders of the _____. (Jam. 5:14)
45. A torn-up piece of material.
48. The Thin Man's wife (Nick and _____).
50. In _____ was there a voice heard. (Matt. 2:18)
51. Poetic for *before*.
52. Walked.
53. I am (contraction).
54. _____ them that love us in the faith. (Titus 3:15)

DOWN CLUES

1. Belonging to Adam's son.
2. English princess.
3. A witty saying.
4. United Nations (abbr.).
5. Take no thought...what ye shall _____. (Luke 12:11)
6. A man _____ God.
7. Metal from mining.
9. He that is _____ days old. (Gen. 17:12)
11. To capture a lawbreaker.
13. A yellow car in New York City.
14. Also.
16. Authority to _____ these things. (Mark 11:28)
19. Firstlings of thy herds _____ of thy flock. (Deut. 12:17)
20. _____ not a servant unto his master. (Prov. 30:10)
21. Now _____ faith, hope, charity. (1 Cor. 13:13)
22. A spool of film.
24. Industrious insects.
26. He was _____ at that saying. (Mark 10:22)
28. Yes (nautical).
29. Sat down to _____ and to drink. (Ex. 32:6)
30. Slight variation in speech patterns.
31. Sheep's sound.
32. New Testament (abbr.).
33. _____ have and _____ hold.
37. _____ with thine adversary quickly. (Matt. 5:25)

38. Type of train.
40. Neither/______ .
41. A heel.
42. Bezaleel the son of ______ .
    (Ex. 38:22)
43. 900 in Roman numerals.

44. A witch is an old ______ .
46. He is, they ______ .
47. And so ______ them up out of the
    land. (Ex. 1:10)
49. Rosemary (nickname).

PUZZLE 12

ACROSS CLUES

1. Los Angeles (abbr.).
3. Paul came to ______. (Acts 18:19)
10. National Basketball Association (abbr.).
12. To make joyful.
13. 3.14159265.
15. Tool for weeding.
17. This is the way, walk ye in ______. (Isa. 30:21)
18. Even ______ Christ forgave you. (Col. 3:13)
19. They...travelled as far as...______. (Acts 11:19)
21. Ehud the son of ______. (Judg. 3:15)
22. Distress signal.
24. ______ not.
25. Where is the king of...______? (2 Kgs. 19:13)
26. Ready...also to ______ at Jerusalem. (Acts 21:13)
28. Cast ______ between me and Jonathan. (1 Sam. 14:42)

30. Catholic service.
31. Over the brook _____.
    (John 18:1)
32. Jacob called Rachel and _____.
    (Gen. 31:4)
34. Mistreat.
37. You (biblical).
38. _____ of the Chaldees. (Gen.
    15:7)
40. Intending after _____ to bring him
    forth. (Acts 12:4)
42. _____ came out to meet Barak.
    (Judg. 4:22)
43. Holland cheese.
44. God _____ loved the world.
    (John 3:16)
45. An unruly crowd.

DOWN CLUES

2. Unknown author (abbr.).
3. Each (abbr.).
4. Art thou _____ that should come?
    (Matt. 11:3)
5. _____ and Semachiah were
    strong men. (1 Chron. 26:7)
6. Jesus...wearied..._____ thus on
    the well. (John 4:6)
7. Western state (abbr.).
8. All flesh shall _____. (Luke 3:6)
9. A relaxing pool.
11. Now Philip was of _____.
    (John 1:44)
14. Belonging to Abraham's son.
15. _____ is the father of Canaan.
    (Gen. 9:18)
16. A person may have many _____
    in his life.
20. We would call Samson a _____.
21. Shall Christ come out of _____?
    (John 7:41)
23. Exclamation.
24. Porcius _____. (Acts 24:27)
25. To make part of a group.
26. Belonging to the man who did not
    fear the lions.
27. Exists.
29. Used to carry other objects.
30. Mother.
33. Belonging to Canaan's son.
    (Gen. 10:15)
35. South America (abbr.).
36. Out of the _____ of Jesse.
    (Isa. 11:1)
39. Take...a _____ for a burnt
    offering. (Lev. 9:2)
41. Adam's _____.
42. *Yes* in German.

PUZZLE 13

ACROSS CLUES

1. Principles.
7. The sword of _____. (Judg. 7:14)
12. An horn of _____ for us. (Luke 1:69)
14. But _____ mightier than I cometh. (Luke 3:16)
15. Consumed.
16. Nor hear your _____. (Matt. 10:14)
17. He is cast into a _____. (Job 18:8)
18. Interational Cooperative Alliance (abbr.).
19. Standing Room Only (abbr.).
20. A disease of the lungs (abbr.).
22. Wind direction.
23. Exclamation of satisfaction.
25. To impose a necessary accompaniment or result.
26. Batters.
29. Negative.
30. Either/ _____.
31. Lamech...begat _____. (Gen. 5:30)
32. Saint (abbr.).
33. A large long-haired Asian animal.
34. The kingdom of _____ in Bashan. (Josh. 13:31)
35. To take _____.
37. Oriental cooking pans.
38. Very wet dirt.
39. I _____ no pleasant bread. (Dan. 10:3)
40. Left Tackle (abbr.).
41. Shalt thou find no _____. (Deut. 28:65)
43. _____, I come to do thy will. (Heb. 10:7)
44. Hairy Southern vegetable.
46. Roman numeral for 550.
47. Lest any of them should _____ out. (Acts 27:42)
49. For I trust _____ _____ you. (Rom. 15:24; 2 words)
50. Lay not this _____ to their charge. (Acts 7:60)
52. In the middle of.
53. Emergency Room (abbr.).
54. Throws.
55. Made...the sea, and all that in them _____. (Acts 4:24)
56. _____ Abram departed. (Gen. 12:4)

DOWN CLUES

1. A prophet.
2. Identical.
3. Request.
4. Audiovisual (abbr.).
5. Abraham...kept...my statutes and my _____. (Gen. 26:5)
6. A person who saves things.
7. They were both righteous before _____. (Luke 1:6)
8. Continuing _____ in prayer. (Rom. 12:12)
9. Long period of time.
10. I have commanded my sanctified _____. (Isa. 13:3)
11. NBC, CBS, ABC.
13. Fill his skin with barbed _____. (Job 41:7)
21. Having to do with a natural science (prefix).
24. Idols.
27. Christ went up _____ Jerusalem.
28. The son of Gera. (Judg. 3:15)
30. A strong wood comes from these.
32. Supersonic Transport (abbr.).

33. Part of an egg (plural).
34. Belonging to the son of Ephlal. (1 Chron. 2:37)
36. Belonging to Ruth's mother-in-law. (Ruth 1:2)
38. Used instead of *Miss* today.
42. _____ _____ lamp (2 words).
43. Citrus fruit.
44. Expression of regret after a mistake.
45. Having to do with airplanes or space.
48. God _____ with the lad. (Gen. 21:20)
51. Yes or _____.

PUZZLE 14

ACROSS CLUES

1. Jonathan _____ up upon his hands. (1 Sam. 14:13)
5. Automobile.
8. The Philistines took the ark...to _____. (1 Sam. 5:1)
11. Belonging to the son of Jephunneh. (Num. 13:6)
14. Lizard, snail, and _____ are unclean. (Lev. 11:30)
15. Much _____ about nothing.
16. He is up _____ _____ good (2 words).
17. Printer's measure.
18. Sea bird.
21. Prefix meaning into.
23. Mother.
25. Thou hast followed _____. (1 Kgs. 18:18)
27. For example.
28. Duty every soldier hates.
29. Take thy neighbour's raiment _____ pledge. (Ex. 22:26)
30. National Football League (abbr.).
32. Good _____ are not everything.
35. Bela the son of _____. (Gen. 36:32)
37. Hello.
38. Fe, _____ Fo, Fum.
39. To exist.
41. The strong hold of _____. (2 Sam. 24:7)
43. To offer a sacrifice unto_____ their god. (Judg. 16:23)
46. What holds up a golf ball.
47. To surprise someone.
49. I am (contr.).
50. There was a marriage in _____ of Galilee. (John 2:1)
52. He killed Goliath.
53. A meat offering baken in a _____. (Lev. 2:5)
54. Ancient wisdom.
55. Rulers of _____. (Ex. 18:21)

DOWN CLUES

2. I _____ in the way of righteousness. (Prov. 8:20)
3. Curley and _____.
4. Emergency Medical Service (abbr.).
5. Them which are of the house of _____. (1 Cor. 1:11)
6. A sweetened fruit drink.
7. Rosemary (abbr.).
8. Thy father was an _____. (Ezek. 16:3)
9. This is my beloved _____. (Matt. 3:17)
10. Spoken of by _____ the prophet. (Matt. 24:15)
11. The excellency of _____ and Sharon. (Isa. 35:2)
12. _____ sat in the gate of Sodom. (Gen. 19:1)
13. Belonging to the son of Abinoam. (Judg. 4:6)
19. Ebenezer (abbr.).
20. Just a little rest.
22. Prefix meaning *not*.
24. Lost three days _____. (1 Sam. 9:20)
26. What a cow says.
31. Fabulous.
33. _____ _____ of little faith. (Matt. 6:3; 2 words, var.)
34. The king carried the people captive to _____. (2 Kgs. 16:9)
35. Said Jehu to _____ his captain. (2 Kgs. 9:25)

36. Joseph and Mary looked for a
_____ _____ an inn. (2 words).
40. Belonging to Gaal's father. (Judg.
9:30)
41. Son of Ishmael. (Gen. 25:13, 15)
42. Joshua built an altar in mount
_____. (Josh. 8:30)
44. Moses gave unto..._____...the
kingdom of Sihon. (Num. 32:33)
45. Part of a cathedral.
46. Given for good service.
48. Ye rebelled...in the desert of
_____. (Num. 27:14)
51. Not *yes*.

PUZZLE 15

ACROSS CLUES

1. Having to do with the Bible.
9. There _____ none good but one. (Mark 10:18)
11. The _____ of March.
12. _____ the money.
13. To utilize.
14. 1,400 in Roman numerals.
15. To drift off to sleep.
16. Your children...received _____ correction. (Jer. 2:30)
17. Old Testament (abbr.).
19. Whom the Father will _____ in my name. (John 14:26)
22. They _____ go the man. (Judg. 1:25)
25. Art not thou a _____? (2 Sam. 15:27)
26. One of the Great Lakes.
27. They came to him from _____ quarter. (Mark 1:45)
29. Paul, a _____ of Jesus Christ. (Rom. 1:1)
30. To raise a child, or to _____ a child.
31. Sound of satisfaction.
32. Manuscript (abbr.).
33. Dad.
35. The harvest is the _____ of the world. (Matt. 13:39)
36. _____ Abram departed. (Gen. 12:4)
37. The one who gets to the finish line first _____ the prize.
39. Alternating Current (abbr.).
41. Israel assembled together at _____. (Josh. 18:1)
42. Policeman's Benevolent Association (abbr.).
43. A tall, flightless bird.
44. Talk-show host.
45. I will come down and _____ with thee. (Num. 11:17)
46. Hear my _____, O God. (Ps. 61:1)
48. They filled them _____ to the brim. (John 2:7)
50. Ye shall not _____ me hence forth. (Matt. 23:39)
51. To _____ away our sins. (1 John 3:5)
52. A crown of twelve _____. (Rev. 12:1)

DOWN CLUES

1. Less complex.
2. Centers for Disease Control (abbr.).
3. God led them by the way of the _____ sea. (Ex. 13:18)
4. God _____ a Spirit. (John 4:24)
5. Also.
6. Does, then _____.
7. I took the little book, and _____ it up. (Rev. 10:10)
8. And, _____, the heavens were opened. (Matt. 3:16)
9. God _____ my strength and power. (2 Sam. 22:33)
10. And _____ rain on the just and on the unjust. (Matt. 5:45)
15. Someone who can't mind his or her own business is _____.
18. "Star _____."
19. Fives, sixes, and _____.
20. Equal Rights Amendment (abbr.).
21. _____, *Pinta*, and *Santa Maria*.
23. Adam's wife.
24. Go, _____, go!
28. Railroads (abbr.).

33. I will even make the ______ for
    fire great. (Ezek. 24:9)
34. Most-quoted author in the world.
36. He made the pure incense of
    ______ spices. (Ex. 37:29)
37. Clever coyote's name.
38. All the people shall ______. (Josh.
    6:5)
39. For God is ______ to make him
    stand. (Rom. 14:4)
40. They baked unleavened ______ of
    the dough. (Ex. 12:39)
41. He made him to ______ honey out
    of the rock. (Deut. 32:13)
42. As the flower of the grass he shall
    ______ away. (Jam. 1:10)
47. About (abbr.).
49. Dad.

PUZZLE 16

ACROSS CLUES

1. Hid from _____ and from generations. (Col. 1:26)
5. _____ is your reward in heaven. (Matt. 5:12)
10. The _____ shall come and take our place. (John 11:48)
12. I will not _____ to speak of any thing. (Rom. 15:18)
14. For example.
15. Missouri.
16. _____ thy son, he shall build my house. (1 Chron. 28:6)
17. David...feigned himself _____. (1 Sam. 21:12,13)
18. _____ I my brother's keeper? (Gen. 4:9)
19. The power of _____. (Es. 1:3)
21. As _____ obeyed Abraham. (1 Pet. 3:6; alt. spelling)
24. How can these things _____? (John 3:9)
25. Truth _____ Consequences.
26. Ambush between Beth-el and _____. (Josh. 8:12)
27. All sailors can tie a _____.
29. An authoritative standard.
31. Into captivity unto _____. (Amos 1:5)
32. Where are the gods of...Hena and _____? (2 Kgs. 18:34)
33. Amos, the son of _____. (Luke 3:25)
35. A middle point between extremes.
36. A unit of dry measure.
38. Above-ground subway.
39. _____ and Bartholomew. (Matt. 10:3)

40. _____, Tekel, Upharsin. (Dan. 5:25)
43. Let us _____ over unto the other side. (Luke 8:22)
44. These _____ght Milcah did bear to Nahor. (Gen. 22:23)
46. Prefix having to do with the earth.
47. I write not these things to _____ you. (1 Cor. 4:14)
51. Simeon that was called _____. (Acts 13:1)
52. In the top of the rock _____. (Judg. 15:8)

DOWN CLUES

1. Height times width.
2. _____ and Magog. (Rev. 20:8)
4. But a certain _____. (Luke 10:33)
6. City in Brazil.
7. Why make ye this _____, and weep? (Mark 5:39)
8. Absalom's sister. (2 Sam. 13:1)
9. As a _____ gathereth her chickens. (Matt. 23:37)
11. Drifts off to sleep.
13. Rome (Ital.).
16. The excellency of Carmel and _____. (Isa. 35:2)
17. Pray ye to the Lord for _____. (Acts 8:24)
19. Jacob called the name of the place _____. (Gen. 32:30)
20. A free electron.
21. Hannah...bare a son, ...called ..._____. (1 Sam. 1:20)
22. They fled before the men of _____. (Josh. 7:4)
23. Speed it up!
24. Book (abbr.).
28. Eggs.

30. Whitewater.
34. 1, 101 in Roman numerals.
35. What the hand wrote on the wall.
    (Dan. 5:25)
37. Kitchen Police (abbr.).
39. Balak brought Balaam unto the
    top of _____. (Num. 23:28)
41. In the white of an _____.
    (Job 6:6)
42. Formerly.
43. Jewel.
45. I am glorified _____ them.
    (John 17:10)
48. Cursed is _____ that curseth thee.
    (Num. 24:9)
49. But also to die _____ Jerusalem.
    (Acts 21:13)
50. Mom.

PUZZLE 17

ACROSS CLUES

1. Expression of satisfaction.
3. Stayed.
8. God heard the voice of the _____. (Gen. 21:17)
9. A prohibition.
10. Mom.
11. One _____ the other.
12. Joseph...entered into his _____. (Gen. 43:30)
15. The child Jesus tarried _____. (Luke 2:43)
18. Drink originally from China.
19. Compass direction.
20. _____ not this folly. (Judg. 19:23)
22. The people sin against _____ Lord. (1 Sam. 14:33)
23. As they that must give _____. (Heb. 13:17)
26. _____ and good. (Gen. 41:5)
27. And they did eat of the _____ corn. (Josh. 5:11)
28. I am (contraction).

32. Set your _____ on things above.
(Col. 3:2)
36. Let not the sun _____ down on
your wrath. (Eph. 4:26)
37. Deliver thyself as a _____ from
the...hunter. (Prov. 6:5)
38. Ribonucleic acid.
39. 2,000 pounds.
40. Larry, Curley, and _____.
42. Their _____ hath been to feed
cattle. (Gen. 46:32)
44. That all men through him might
_____. (John 1:7)
46. What a boat needs if it has no
motor.
47. Estimated Time of Arrival
(abbr.).
48. Of your daily _____. (Ex. 5:19)
49. Added to a word to make it an
adverb.

DOWN CLUES

1. Rabbits.
2. Not *B.C.*
3. The _____ of their joy.
(2 Cor. 8:2)
4. What a sheep says.
5. Incorporated (abbr.).
6. English noblewoman.
7. 3 measures of _____ for a penny.
(Rev. 6:6)
8. Part of the ear or brain.

10. He walked with _____.
(Mal. 2:6)
13. In a certain place.
14. When kings go forth to _____.
(2 Sam. 11:1)
16. Ye therefore _____ them not.
(John 8:47)
17. A place to tie a boat.
21. He that is of _____ heareth.
(John 8:47)
24. There had been _____ rain.
(1 Kgs. 17:7)
25. Hello!
29. Former Chinese leader.
30. Take ye a kid of the _____ for a
sin offering. (Lev. 9:3)
31. Full of dead men's _____.
(Matt. 23:27)
33. Guy, pal, a good _____.
34. All the _____ of the field are
withered. (Joel 1:12)
35. Not out.
36. Reverence and _____ fear.
(Heb. 12:28)
37. They put on Jesus a scarlet
_____. (Matt. 27:28)
39. Take it by the _____. (Ex. 4:4)
40. Martha...went and _____ him.
(John 11:20)
41. Eggs.
43. Egyptian god.
45. "Entertainment Tonight" (abbr.).

PUZZLE 18

Diana Rowland

ACROSS CLUES

1. Son of God.
6. The book of the generation of Jesus _____. (Matt. 1:1)
12. Nebuzar-_____, captain of the guard, _____ servant. (2 Kgs. 25:8; 2 words)
13. Thou mayest prosper and be in _____. (3 John 2)
14. And flee into _____. (Matt. 2:13)
15. Published throughout all his _____. (Es. 1:20)
16. Behold, there came a _____. (Matt. 8:2)
17. I have given _____ unto the children of Lot. (Deut. 2:9)
18. Knockout (abbr.).
19. _____, the chamberlain of the city. (Rom. 16:23)
22. Blessed are the pure _____ heart. (Matt. 5:8)
23. _____ it is not _____. (Acts 22:22; 2 words)
25. If ye then, _____ evil. (Matt. 7:11)
27. Did _____ _____ lightness?... that with _____. (2 Cor. 1:17; 3 words)
28. Put off all these; _____, wrath. (Col. 3:8)
30. Party after a wedding.
33. Do, _____, Mi.
34. In the very _____. _____ Moses...us, _____. (John 8:4,5; 3 words)
36. The sons of Caleb, _____, Elah, and Naam. (1 Chron. 4:15)
37. Day after Monday (abbr.).
38. By faith, _____, being warned of God. (Heb. 11:7)
41. City that is _____ on a hill. (Matt. 5:14)
42. And when the _____ heard it. (Matt. 20:24)
43. Whosoever shall _____ me before men. (Matt. 10:33)
44. They did all _____. (Matt. 14:20)
47. As a _____ lappeth. (Judg. 7:5)
49. The son of _____. (Luke 3:36)
50. Let your light _____ shine. (Matt. 5:16)
51. They may appear unto men _____ fast. (Matt. 6:16)
52. Registered Nurse (abbr.).

DOWN CLUES

1. _____ went out to meet Sisera. (Judg. 4:18)
2. Fall by the _____ of the sword. (Luke 21:24)
3. But I _____ unto you...use you, and _____ you. (Matt. 5:44; 2 words)
4. My substance, yet being _____. (Ps. 139:16)
5. And _____ upon it...his _____ white as snow. (Matt. 28:2,3; 2 words)
6. Every _____ had two faces. (Ezek. 41:18)
7. Touched the _____ of his garment. (Matt. 9:20)
8. Hit sharply.
9. _____ fear my lord...your faces worse _____. (Dan. 1:10; 2 words)
10. Weakness of God is _____ than men. (1 Cor. 1:25)
11. Blessed are _____ merciful. (Matt. 5:7)

17. Heaven is _____ hand.
    (Matt. 3:2)
20. If my _____ hath turned _____ of
    the way. (Job 31:7; 2 words,
    reverse order)
21. _____(h) Zidon: for the _____
    hath spoken. (Isa. 23:4; reversed)
23. Fe, _____, Fo, Fum.
24. For _____ lamps _____ gone out.
    (Matt. 25:8; 2 words)
26. Brought him to an _____, _____.
    (Luke 10:34; 2 words)
29. Do, _____, Mi.
31. Wool fabric.
32. Groweth of _____ own...shalt

_____ reap. (Lev. 25:5; 2 words)
35. As the _____ of the feet.
    (Dan. 2:42)
36. Theirs _____ the kingdom of
    heaven. (Matt. 5:3)
39. _____, Eshcol, and Mamre.
    (Gen. 14:24)
40. And when they had sung an
    _____. (Matt. 26:30)
45. Ye shall be _____ gods.
    (Gen. 3:5)
46. Think not that I am come _____
    destroy the law. (Matt. 5:17)
48. _____ and search diligently.
    (Matt. 2:8)

PUZZLE 19

ACROSS CLUES

1. Works, which were _____ in you. (Matt. 11:21)
5. Him and _____.
8. Kimberly (nickname).
10. This...sinful _____. (Mark 8:38)
12. Her countenance was no more _____. (1 Sam. 1:18)
13. Set it up there under an _____. (Josh. 24:26)
14. Whose waters cast up mire and _____. (Isa. 57:20)
17. Emergency Medical Technician (abbr.).
18. _____ and mercy shall follow me. (Ps. 23:6)
20. Shed _____ blood. (Gen. 37:22)
21. There shall be _____ poor among you. (Deut. 15:4)
22. Ye have _____ portion...in Jerusalem. (Neh. 2:20)
25. Audiovisual (abbr.).
26. Large tree, largely destroyed by blight.

28. Though now ye ______ him not.
(1 Pet. 1:8)
29. From my youth ______.
(Luke 18:21)
30. They that handle the ______.
(Judg. 5:14)
31. Love is the ______ of the law.
(Rom. 13:10)
36. Not out.
37. Support group for those who quit
drinking.
38. Prefix meaning *new*.
39. Coming to him and ______ him
vinegar. (Luke 23:36)
43. I...quieted myself, as a child,
______ ______ weaned child.
(Ps. 131:2; 2 words)
44. Actual.
45. Saint (abbr.).
46. Tenant farmer in the Middle
Ages.
47. Esau ______ Jacob. (Gen. 27:41)

DOWN CLUES

2. Bashan was ruled by king
______. (Deut. 3:1)
3. Bring the offering...of the ______
wine. (Neh. 10:39)
4. Printer's measure.
5. See that ye ______ the matter.
(2 Chron. 24:5)
6. Estimated Time of Arrival
(abbr.).

7. Jumps on his horse and ______.
8. Something a sailor is good at.
9. Maketh (mod.).
11. Go on before ______. (1 Sam.
25:19)
14. He that is mighty hath ______ ...
great things. (Luke 1:49)
15. Set...the ______...in the house of
God. (2 Chron. 33:7)
16. Registered Nurse (abbr.).
18. Ye shall be brought before ______
and kings. (Matt. 10:18)
19. Ship's cry of distress.
20. To sleep for a little while.
23. Stretching forth thine hand to
______. (Acts 4:30)
24. In thy presence is ______ of joy.
(Ps. 16:11)
27. Tooth.
32. The unfeigned ______ that is in
thee. (2 Tim. 1:5)
33. But if we walk in the ______. (1
John 1:7)
34. "Are you coming?"
" ______ ______ minute" (2 words).
35. He shall set the ______ on the left.
(Matt. 25:33)
40. Charge for professional services.
41. To be with Christ; which is
______ better. (Phil. 1:23)
42. Small imaginary being.

PUZZLE 20

ACROSS CLUES

1. Johoiada was leader of the _____.
   (1 Chron. 12:27)
7. A serviceman who did not return
   from war may be one of these.
9. To forbid.
10. Learn to _____ well. (Isa. 1:17)
11. Abraham would be called this
    today.
13. Remember what _____ did.
    (Deut. 25:17)
16. A wise guy.
18. Speak unto...Israel, that they
    _____ forward. (Ex. 14:15)
20. He will _____ a wild man.
    (Gen. 16:12)
21. Familiar form of *you* in
    German.
22. _____ the son of Ner.
    (2 Sam. 3:25)
23. Parts of a play.

25. Sons of Zeruiah, Joab, Abishai,
and _____. (2 Sam. 2:18)
27. Saint (abbr.).
28. Extol him...by his name _____.
(Ps. 68:4)
29. Compass direction.
31. All the _____ and strangers.
(Acts 17:21)
34. Judah and _____. (Jer. 9:26)
36. For example (abbr.).
37. Thou shalt not..._____.
(Lev. 19:13)
39. Elevation (abbr.).
41. The name thereof is called_____.
(Ezek. 20:29)
44. _____ and Caiaphas being high
priests. (Luke 3:2)
46. Captains over _____. (Deut. 1:15)
47. 1,001 in Roman numerals.
48. Carried them captive to _____.
(2 Kgs. 15:29)
49. From _____ to Beer-sheba.
(Judg. 20:1)

DOWN CLUES

1. Belonging to Nabal's wife
(1 Sam. 25:3)
2. Antiaircraft (abbr.).
3. Ribonucleic acid (abbr.).
4. Not working.
5. Upon the great _____ of their
right foot. (Ex. 29:20)
6. South America (abbr.).
7. The sound a kitten makes.
8. A decree from Caesar _____.
(Luke 2:1)
12. The beginning of his kingdom
was _____. (Gen. 10:10)
14. Sarah died...and _____ came to
mourn. (Gen. 23:2)
15. King Saul's father.
(1 Sam. 10:21)
17. Fruit drinks.
19. Obstetrician (abbr.).
24. Chemical Engineer (abbr.).
26. And Leah...called his name
_____. (Gen. 30:13)
30. _____ are labourers together with
God. (1 Cor. 3:9)
32. _____, id, superego.
33. The young men of _____.
(Ezek. 30:17)
35. Made silver shrines for _____.
(Acts 19:24)
38. Passing through the valley of
_____. (Ps. 84:6)
40. An Eastern monk.
41. To _____ or not to be. ·
42. Manuscripts (abbr.).
43. The _____ is withered away.
(Isa. 15:6)
45. Which taketh away the _____ of
the world. (John 1:29)
46. Their cry came up _____ God.
(Ex. 2:23)

PUZZLE 21

ACROSS CLUES

1. Let him deny _____ and take up his cross. (Mark 8:34)
6. _____ Lincoln.
9. Spirit of the Lord came up____ David. (1 Sam. 16:13)
10. Being exceedingly _____ against them. (Acts 26:11)
12. We.
13. _____, and also our fathers. (Gen. 46:34)
14. Tower, whose _____ may reach unto heaven. (Gen. 11:4)
16. Defeats.
22. Environmental Protection Agency (abbr.).
23. To and _____.
24. The _____ was upon the earth forty days. (Gen. 7:12)
28. Take the widow's ox for a _____. (Job 24:3)
30. Tool for weeding.
31. Mary anointed the Lord with _____. (John 11:2)
33. God gave them up unto _____ affections. (Rom. 1:26)
35. New Testament (abbr.).
36. United States (abbr.).
37. Mary _____ Joseph.
38. And thine _____ as the grass of the earth. (Job 5:25)
41. Is able to.
43. Is the correct size.
44. Hereafter ye shall _____ heaven open. (John 1:51)
46. A grain.
47. As he is Christ's, even _____ are we Christ's. (2 Cor. 10:7)
48. Pound (abbr.).
50. Mother.
51. Yea.
52. Teach us to _____ our days. (Ps. 90:12)

DOWN CLUES

1. A prophet is not without _____. (Matt. 13:57)
2. Not out.
3. O thou _____, go. (Amos 7:12)
4. 950 in Roman numerals.
5. Do, re, me, _____.
7. Unclean animal. (Deut. 14:18)
8. It _____ not good (Gen. 2:18)
11. And to _____ is gain. (Phil. 1:21)
12. Jesus went _____ to Jerusalem.
13. For _____ are his workmanship. (Eph. 2:10)
15. Remember all thy _____. (Ps. 20:3)
17. Christian Era (abbr.).
18. The Lord heard...and looked on ...our _____. (Deut. 26:7)
19. Sickness (French).
20. He was _____ at that saying. (Mark 10:22)
21. One of the king's most _____ princess. (Es. 6:9)
25. What every director hopes for.
26. Charged particle.
27. Cast the _____ on the right side. (John 21:6)
29. Be not among...riotous _____ of flesh. (Prov. 23:20)
31. _____ top of that....
32. Something worn to warm the ears or hands.
33. A form of car.
34. 450 in Roman numerals.
38. I have commanded my sanctified _____. (Isa. 13:3)

39. Physical therapy (abbr.).
40. A group of people working for a common cause.
41. Hear, O Lord, when I ______.
    (Ps. 27:7)
42 *Yes*, in the navy.
45. Printer's measure.
48. Pound (abbr.).
49. To exist.

ANSWERS

PUZZLE 1

```
P   B E T H L E H E M
U P E   O E D   I   E R
S A L E M   R   N     E
    R   R   O B A D I A H
I T   S E E   P       U
    H   H I M   H A Y   M
S I R E N   R O T S     S
    A   B   P A   A   B
O N   A B I M E L E C H
I S     A N   I     E A
L   T A R S U S   N O T
S   H   A     O R   H E
M E   K E T U R A H   G
```

PUZZLE 2

```
G A D   O O P S   B R A Y
O N E   F R E E   R O B E
D N A   F E E D   O D E S
S A R A I   L E S T
      A C T   R A H A B S
A T V   E V E   T E R A H
C H E M   S A D   R A R E
T R I E S   T I N   M E M
S U N S E T   P A Y
        S P U D   T E P I D
T H A I   B A T H   A D E
I O T A   A R E A   N E A
S E T S   L E A N   G A D
```

PUZZLE 3

```
P R O P H E T   C A L E B
H O W   O R E   A L O N E
A M   M A T R I   T O N
R A M S E S   N J   S O
I N   I S   T O   O T   N
S   S T   B E   S S   S I
E L I   K E N I T E S
E O N   I N   T O P L A N
  N   D J S   W H E N
A G O   R A M S   S E N T
M   N A O M I   P   P A R
E E L   N I T R I C
N A Y S   N E A T   F O E
```

PUZZLE 4

```
A   J O S H U A     B   N
G O O N   A S   A T E N O
O   B E   G   E X O D U S
    P   A G A   U   M E
S E N N A C H E R I B
    T O   I   P   N E T
J O H N   R   H     R
U   I   G E N E S I S
D O O R   V   S I
A   P A L   K I N G S
H   I   O A T   A   A M
  G A L A T I A N S   M Y
N O   A M E N   S O N S
```

PUZZLE 5

PUZZLE 6

PUZZLE 7

PUZZLE 8

PUZZLE 9

PUZZLE 10

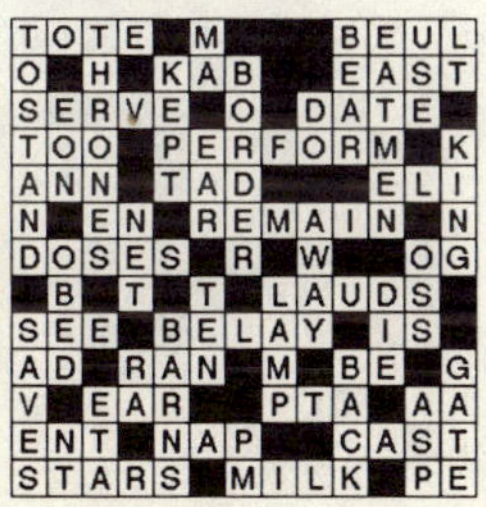

PUZZLE 11

PUZZLE 12

PUZZLE 13

PUZZLE 14

PUZZLE 15

PUZZLE 16

PUZZLE 17

```
 HA  ABIDED    B
LAD  BAN    A  MA
OR   U  CHAMBER  L
BEHIND    TEA   L
ESE   DO  G   THE
   A  ACCOUNT  Y
H  RANK  D  OLD
IM   C    G   E  B
 AFFECTION   GO
ROE     RNA   TON
O  L  MOE  TRADE
BELIEVE  SAILS
ETA  TASK    LY
```

PUZZLE 18

```
JESUS    CHRIST
ADANA    HEALTH
EGYPT    EMPIRE
LEPER  AR   KO
   ERASTUS   IN
FORFIT   BEING
IUSEME   ANGER
RECEPTION   RE
 ACTNOWTHAT
IRU  TUES  NOAH
SET   TEN  DENY
   EAT  DOG  SEMN
   SO    TO    RN
```

PUZZLE 19

```
DONE   HER  KIM
 GENERATION  A
M  W   SAD  OAK
E  DIRT  EMT   E
 GOODNESS  S  S
NO  NO  NO  H  F
AV ELM  SEE  UP
PEN   O    A  L
 R  FULFILLING
IN   AA  I  NEO
 OFFERING  ASA
 REAL  T  H  ST
 SERF  HATED  S
```

PUZZLE 20

```
AARONITES  MIA
BAN    DO  ABE  U
I  AMALEK  AWAG
GO   BE  I  B  DU
ABNER   SCENES
I   ASAHEL  STU
L  JAHS  S    U
SW  ATHENIANS
 EDOM  EG  V
  I   ROBEL  EL
 BAMAH   ANNAS
TENS  A   C  MI
O  ASSYRIA  DAN
```

PUZZLE 21

```
HIMSELF  ABE  I
ONE  MAD  A  US
N  WE   I  TOP
OVERCOMES  F  N
U  EPA  A  FRO
RAIN  PLEDGE  B
 HOE  R  A  R  L
OINTMENT  VILE
NT  US  E  AND
  OFFSPRING  T
CAN  FITS  SEE
RYE  SO  LB  MA
YES   NUMBER  M
```

Published by Barbour and Company, Inc.
                P.O. Box 719
                Uhrichsville, Ohio 44683